Meteor Showers and Us

Meteor Showers
and Us
Poems for speaking aloud
in school and home

Brien Masters

British Library Cataloguing in Publication Data
Masters, Brien
  Meteor Showers and us: poems for speaking aloud
  in school and home.
  I. Title
  821′.914

  ISBN 0-904693-20-1

  Typeset by DP Photosetting, Aylesbury, Bucks
  Printed by The Camelot Press, Southampton

Contents

Proem

The 'cart and horse' approach to education sets out first to arouse and establish understanding, then to harness the understanding to the will and finally to heave, so to speak, in the direction of '... is making satisfactory progress'! Even some toys could be said to be designed to develop *understanding*, though it may appear otherwise. For instance, the toy consisting of some version or other of having to hammer a peg into a hole of equivalent size and shape is obviously of this type.

The other approach may be characterised as the 'hare and tortoise'. Here is not meant the *only* other; but, for present purposes, the simple contrast of two approaches is being presented in order to come comparatively quickly to the point. In this approach, the will is recognised in its full potential, and is stimulated to go 'haring' ahead, either in those early years of childhood when creative play holds the field in a way that is never repeated in later life, or in later stages of schooling, when the understanding, still bleary-eyed from its childhood sleep, has begun to awaken.

In this second educational approach, the will has been unleashed and is well ahead, and in this way stimulates the understanding to catch up. Moreover, there is no second tortoise (as in the original fable of 'The Hare and the Tortoise') waiting to pop up perkily at the finishing post. So the understanding can only plod on, making clear to itself what the will has already mastered.

The recitation of poetry is, educationally speaking, in this category. Rhythmically—in chorus or as a 'solo'—a poem is spoken aloud (recited). In the poem, concepts are contained and concealed of which even the poet himself may often have become no more than intuitively aware. Frequently, the beauty of the poem and its aesthetic attraction lies in its clandestine allusions, its symbolic meaning or its hinted at depths, all of these being clothed in the poetically artistic elements of rhythm, assonance, repetitions, imagery and figures of speech. The last may even include whole string-of-pearl sequences of metaphor.

What the will can grasp immediately in well-formed speech, has to be striven for by the understanding over a period of time. Sometimes the striving is life-long.

In education, Rudolf Steiner recommended that, before even hearing a poem for the first time, the pupils receive a verbal introduction that prepares them for it. This need only be brief. Yet, through it, the understanding is sufficiently awakened to be interested in the forthcoming race (to stay with the metaphor) and will at least know in which direction to set off. Steiner makes the point that, once this has happened, work on the *artistic* nature of the poem can 'go ahead' unhindered. In this connection, the notes at the back for various poems, may give teachers ideas for such introductions, though they also indicate important poetic elements—such as the vowel sequence in 'The Donkey's Journey' (no. 8) or the deliberate change from anapaest (vv—) to iambus v— in 'Sheep Bell' (no. 40). However, teachers' *own* findings are not only equally valid: they are usually more effective educationally. All teachers will have memories of those occasions when they were really able to feed the class with a fresh meal, filled with educational nutrition; equally, few will be unable to recall those occasions when there was at least one item on the menu that was merely 'warmed up'.

Now, a great deal of education, particularly in adolescence, needs to be of the 'horse and cart' type: applying a chemical formula, for example, or translating a passage from the Mother Tongue into a foreign language. Consequently, the other approach can easily be neglected, thereby atrophying both will and intellect. Much of the controversy over religious education is connected with this. In former ages there was hardly any qualmishness over teaching religion by first 'drumming it in', catechistically. (We shall not discuss here what the 'it' refers to or what it is that the 'it' is being drummed into!) Also, here, nothing for or against a catechistic approach to religious education is necessarily being advocated. Yet even at the humble level of plain 'good manners', most parents and teachers begin training these by adopting the 'hare and tortoise' attitude of 'Do this ...', hopefully reflecting in their own behaviour what they admonish and not merely remaining at the (hypocritical?) level of preaching. Where discipline is one of the most urgent debates of the day, this approach deserves full consideration.

Returning to recitation. Emphasis has been given to the different benefits and applications of the two approaches in order to help overcome the not infrequently heard objection to the recitation of poetry (referring to children, that is): 'But do they *understand* it?' (As if everything had to be as plain as a pike-staff.) And it is unlikely that the leanings of a Minister of Education* will 'hold the bridge' for long, unless he can show convincingly that

* The Rt. Hon. Kenneth Baker's outspokenness, towards the end of his term of office, in favour of poetry recitation as an important part of the pupil's curriculum experience, has been a welcome addenda following the Education Reform Act of 1988.

there is real educational substance to support his views, substance with which teachers themselves can freely and whole-
heartedly identify.

A further question would be: How can such poetry recitation
be integrated into the school day? Here one can see how
beneficial it is to follow the model of the Waldorf Main Lesson.
This, as many will be aware, concentrates on one topic over a
period of some 28 days, for about two hours per day. This
generous time factor allows for a several-faceted approach, in
which the recitation can be, and often is, closely and carefully
linked in with the subject being studied. Many of the poems in
sections 2, 3 and 4 of the present collection fall into this category.
Equally well, the mood of each season can be dwelt on—the
poems of section 1 presenting opportunities for this—thereby
enabling the child to become more 'in tune' with the seasonal
environment, to be stimulated by its constantly changing variety
and yet given a sense of security by its unfailingly cyclical return.
Always assuming that the teacher has chosen an appropriate topic
for the Main Lesson, all of this provides a healthy framework in
which the learning process has sufficient 'space' to achieve its
optimum. The foregoing applies to the *group* as a whole. A further
benefit derived from recitation—more for the *individual*—is as
follows. It can best be seen perhaps, by referring to the well
established Waldorf approach to the teaching of modern lan-
guages, which already commences in the Kindergarten and is
purely oral.

It is not only in Waldorf circles that the 'direct approach' to
modern language teaching is regarded as the one which develops
fluency, through an *active* use of the language, more effectively
than the method favoured earlier in the century, which was
predominantly a structured sequence of grammar-based text-
book exercises. It has been demonstrated that, provided the
transition to an *awareness* of the grammar and other structural
elements in the language be made at the right time, the oral or
'direct' approach does not result in less, but more able grammar-
ians, translators, interpreters, linguaphiles and so on. The early
use of the language provides something like a firm buttress which
can provide a reliable support for the grammatical structure to
follow. Without this support, the learning of a language can be
heavy going for children. Given the additional buttresses,
however, the pupils can take the weight of grammar, syntax and
vocabulary learning much more readily on their shoulders. (A
comparison could be made between the experience of *light* in a
Romanesque cathedral such as Durham with that of one built in

Perpendicular style such as York. Durham's solid pillars [of understanding] represent the grammar-taking-the-lead approach; whereas York's light-filled interior [the delight of 'O yes, I've known that all my life'] represents the '*use*-of-the-language-first'—the 'direct approach'. Naturally, this is not to state any preference for the one or the other architectural styles per se; it is only the experience of the *light within* that is being used for comparison.)

The parallel case of the Mother Tongue now becomes clear. For with the Mother Tongue, the language has already been experienced for some years, normally long before the child enters school. At the same time, one cannot assume that the child's understanding has been 'tortoising' along during the same period. For understanding is connected with a form of consciousness that awakens only in later childhood and particularly in adolescence. Therefore with poetry, in the Mother Tongue, the understanding is left far behind if the class recites from an early age. Yet why not? All the more incentive for the understanding once it 'gets going' to bestir itself.

Hence, Steiner education places great emphasis upon the pupils' acquisition of oral skills—both passive (the teacher's presentation of material) and active (the pupils' daily contribution to extended discussion, as well as their regular participation in group recitation, as here being recommended). That is to say, one of the most advanced skills with which the pupil enters school—the *use* of the Mother Tongue—becomes one of the first and most important 'tools' of education. By strategically placing the recitation near the beginning of each Main Lesson, each *individual* pupil (albeit as part of the group—with the attendant *social* advantage that attaches to choral work) is eased daily into this oral stream, as effectively as possible.

The above is probably sufficient—particularly for the modern protagonists of the acquisition of 'communication skills'—to substantiate the view that speaking poetry aloud is educational time well spent; better spent, moreover, the better it is positioned within the school day.

Fortunately there will be those who also regard poetry as something worthwhile in its own right, needing no other recommendation than that it is part of every child's cultural heritage. Or there will be those who recite with their pupils for the purpose of improving articulation, who use it for rhythmic movement of one kind or another, as an essential ingredient of teacher training or for other educational purposes. A poet can only look on gratefully as such people rally around the pennon of the bard.

Additionally, in education, the *right use* of poetry is also something to be studied and practised, lest the whole endeavour misfire or—worse—become counter-productive. It is to assist this right usage that these preliminary words are written.

As in the previous publication (*Weft for the Rainbow* by Brien Masters, The Lanthorn Press, East Grinstead, 1983), I warmly acknowledge the inspiring talents (and needs) of all the pupils and classes for whom the large majority of the poems and verses in the present collection have been written; I trust they will be happy to 'join' those who may receive inspiration through using the poetry in their life and work. It is to this whole company that I address these final words of dedication.

Brien Masters
Michael Hall
July 1989

1
Watching the year— festivals and seasons

METEOR SHOWERS AND US

Meteor showers, luminous in the sky,
As through the unploughed fields
             of speeding-space they ply;

Meteor showers, heralds of sun's light,
Bearing hues of rich coronal splendour
             in their livery bright;

Meteor showers, flinging wide the Tauric gate
As flashing trails of fire,
             in frenzied heaven-sped spate;

Meteor showers, festive in the summer night,
As Michaël's hosts approach,
             their new-forged word to plight;

Meteor showers, hurling down to earth,
Like man from Paradise expelled,
             freedom to bring to birth;

Meteor showers, burning through the void,
Like the iron-red pulse within—
             in sacrifice destroyed;

Meteor showers, imploding in the air,
Like deeds from man's resolves,
             love from prayer;

Meteor showers, chondrites rushing, hissing down,
Trampling on coils of hate—fear, anxiety
             in courage to drown;

Meteor showers, radiant and pure,
Calling on us: Life's challenge
             to endure.

MICHAELMAS SONG

Michaël, riding the Heavens,
Carrying sword and shield;
Horses and ploughman, servants of earth,
    Turning the furrowed field.

Michaël, mast of the mind,
Sailing in oceans of light;
Help us to vanquish the serpent beneath
    And scatter the mists of night.

Michaël, guide to the Sun,
Giver of Life above;
Calling Mankind to waken within
    And serve the Lord of Love.

BRIDGE BUILDING

Bridgeless estuary—deep-gulfed, mud-merged expanse; unfordable;
Bridgeless chasm—like love-forsaken heart-cold; callous, confounding;
Bridgeless falls—death-threatening, devil-dyked; divorcing;
Bridgeless morass—spanless peat-soddened pulp; like bloat-bellied
                          yawning boredom.

Life-saving maths—against gust-galed, hurricaned violence;
Mind-vast plans—with concrete, rock-bedded anchorage;
Caisson manoev'ring—for navvy-shovelling excavators;
Pile-spiked piers—for crane-crested tower-topping girders;
Cable-catenary—with vertical, steel suspenders;
Bascules raised—saluting strength and sacrifice.

Bright spear of Michaël—bridging minds to thoughts of light;
Grasped spear of Michaël—bridging hands to deeds of strength;
Raised spear of Michaël—bridging hearts to words of warmth;
Hurled spear of Michaël—bridging man to Man and God.

HARVEST LOAF

Fields of corn coloured gold by the harvest sun
    Are cut and gathered in;
Sacks of flour, ground and weighed and tied are stacked,
    Midst the miller's merry din;

Tins of dough, mixed and baked, till crusted brown
    Are cooled for loaf and life;
Then sliced and served and blessed and spread,
    Giving strength for joy or strife.

ST MARTIN

St Martin, mounted on his shining steed,
Rode by with flowing cloak and girded sword;
The down-cast beggar, with beseeching eye
And hand in hope uplifted, stumbled forth;
The rider's glance fell softly on the pain-wracked
Figure. Tight the knight brought horse to halt
And, taking cloak and sword, he slit in two
The costly garment, wrapping lovingly
The goose-fleshed shoulders, starved with autumn's cold.

ARUM ET ROSA

Fertile fields of heaven,
Where lilies ever bloom,
Let your light o'erflow
Upon the wintry earth;
     Light from heavenly heights to shine
     In earth's deepest gloom,
     Borne on angel's wing,
     With message of new birth.

Mary's mantle blue,
Rose-royal robe of red,
Angel's wing unfurled
In noiseless depth of soul;
     Purest maiden richly born,
     As purest blossom wed,
     Sun and moon receive now
     And stars from night's deep bowl.

Lily's delicate stem,
Poised in Gabriel's hand,
Maid with inturned gaze,
Trembling in her heart;
     As lily petal blooms and fades,
     God on earth will stand,
     Eternity wedding time
     Whom sin had thrust apart.

Hay in manger waits,
Oxen's noble breath,
Ass, from jogging journey,
Kneels at midnight hour;
     Sun, nestling in crib-wood.
     Crowned with sharp-scythed, hay-gold death;
     Earth the fertile cradle,
     Rose in lily's bower.

GOOD TIDINGS AT YULE

Blizzards blow on Viking skin,
Axe hacks oak for Yule to begin;
Candle in the candle-socket, firm as rock,
Folk fetching greenery at crow of cock;
Box and bay, with the spike-leafed holly—
Red-berried sprigs to banish melancholy;
Green-needled sprays of Norwegian spruce,
Bunches of sage for the fat, stuffed goose;
A nosegay of rosemary, scenting all the fun,
Midst the boar's head, bristling like rays of the sun;
Baldur's bough, cut on its white spread cloth,
Wine on the log to appease Thor's wrath;
    Past the winter solstice;
    Darkness disdain;
    For the King of the carol,
    The King of the dance.
    The King of the Elements,
    From realms of light
    Has come to reign.

Sinewy hands haul the ivy-twined ropes,
Kindling Yule's threshold with ash-healing hopes;
Feast-trestles groan with the gruel and cake
And bowls of steaming mead for the thirsts still to slake;
Thumb unblemished feels the carver's blade
By dish of spitted beast on the scrubbed board laid;
Cornelians wink from the torch-lit brooch
As the cloaks furl to rest at the feast-lords' approach;
Dragon-prows silently heaving on the firth,
Swords unbuckled at the Sun's rebirth:
'Gather now and hearken, ye who've had your fill,
For peace is on earth to men of good will.'
    Past the winter solstice;
    Darkness disdain;
    For the King of the carol,
    The King of the dance,
    The King of the Elements,
    From realms of light
    Has come to reign.

THREE MOTHERS

Mother Earth in days of Eden,
Streams of flowing life abounding,
Trees of plenty bending earthwards,
Fruit and birdsong fill your branches;
All your creatures God obey:
    In my heart that garden's glory,
    Roses red in full array.

Mother Eve at Eden's gateway,
Thrust of fiery sword expels her,
Banished into outer darkness,
Through the taste which serpent tempted,
For the fruit forbidden:
    In my heart a welcome for her,
    Where warmth and light lie hidden.

Mother Mary wends through starland,
Gathering threads to weave her mantle;
Through the love she bears within her,
Thorns of Eden turn to roses
For the Christ-Child's birth:
    In my heart, Thou child of Heaven,
    Bring Paradise on earth.

THE DONKEY'S JOURNEY

Donkey who strode
    Where the stream flowed
Lightening the load
Of Mary who rode.

Journey so hard
    Doors were all barred
Room by the yard
Neath the sky starred.

Inn-keeper's pride
    In stable abide
God be your guide
Joseph and bride.

Burden is freed
    Where cattle feed
Shepherds take heed
To Bethlem with speed.

Maiden who prayed
    While Gabriel stayed
Lily arrayed
Be not afraid.

Cattle that chewed
    Sweet hay their food
Turtle-dove cooed
By the crib rude.

Kneel with heads bowed
    Sun casts no cloud
Heart's joy sing loud
Dance through the crowd.

THREE KINGS

Kneeling in the Christ-Child's beauty,
Cradled in his warmth and light,
Filled with flowing peace their feelings
Darkness turned to heart-joy bright.

Clad in mantles richly broidered,
Jewelled gifts to Him they bring;
Dome-gold crowns their heads adorning,
Heart's o'er-flowing offering,
　　　Reverent silence filled with angels,
　　　Winging singing for their king.

　　　Bowing farewell the kings leave Him with dignity,
　　　Turning to worlds of star and spur,
　　　Astride their steeds prancing in stately procession,
　　　Carrying joy's tidings into the year.

Mounted they ride in star-leading majesty,
The twinkling heavens floating in waters deep,
'Twixt red day burning on desert sand-dune
And ice-crystal frozen on mountain steep;
　　　Till each striving heart is cloaked with their velvet,
　　　Giving spur to each day, and light through sleep.

ST BRIDE OF IONA

The trail treads she to the trembling rowan tree:
Rowan tree trembling—
Treads trail—
With bright glowing reds in the brimful blue;
Blue brimful—
Reds glowing bright.

The track treads she of the trade-tired merchant;
Merchant trade-tired—
Treads track—
In the courtyard, cluttered with sand-dusted saddle-bags:
Saddle-bags sand-dusted—
Cluttered courtyard.

She gently treads in the straw-hushed shelter:
Shelter straw-hushed—
Treads gently—
And sings the babe lullabies 'neath velvet star-bowl:
Star-bowl velvet—
Lullabies babe.

DAWN CHORUS

Birds in the dawn
Dawn in the joy of birds
    Thrill in the air
    Air in the full-feathered thrill
        Song in the sun
        Sun in the chorus of song

Leaf in the bush
Bush in the bounty of leaf
    Spring in the briar
    Briar in the bursting spring
        Green in the trees
        Trees in the chorus of green

Light in the stars
Stars in the showering of light
    Peace in the sleep
    Sleep in the voices of peace
        Night in the heavens
        Heavens in the chorus of night

Day in the world
World in the waking of day
    Man in the void
    Void in the challenge of Man
        Life in the soul
        Soul in the chorus of life

PASS OVER

(On receiving three post cards: A Sisley, a Turner and a Grünewald)

I saw an Autumn tree,
Whose brittle leaves in summer fire,
With bugle breath,
Defying death,
Ablaze within my soul did me enthrall.

I saw on mountain slope,
By avalanche's fury crumbled,
A shepherd's cot,
In hope begot,
Mingled stone and splintered pine asprawl.

I saw a mother's tear
From cheek to cold earth softly fall:
Yet night's dark sway
Must fold away
When Easter Sun in depths of soul doth call.

JOSEPH OF ARIMATHEA

Gold-shafted glade
Fields of spring joy
Flooded with Easter-filled morning-spun light
Awaken
In silence
Each chalice
Frost challenged—
Flow life!
Freed from the fetters of night
Freed from the night!

Sepulchre cool
Spear-guarded peace
Lit by the Easter-dawn garden-fresh glow
Dew sprinkled
Sun dancing
Moon rising
Rock shattering—
Faith's joy!
Loyal to the last despite foe
Loyal despite foe.

Vanquished is fear
Table is set
Fed by the Easter-raised life-giving sun
In darkness
Sustaining
No prison
Holds peril—
Soul strength!
Spirit of victory won
Victory won.

Forth to new lands
Emperor-freed
Led by the Easter-born vessel of gold
Disciple
Spear sun-raised
I come now
Shame ransomed—
Ride crests!
Forward to kingdoms untold
Kingdoms untold.

THE KNIGHT STAINED FROM BATTLE

Who is he, this lordling young, that cometh from the fight?
With blood-red raiment disarrayed from putting foe to flight,
With fair apparel, crowned with stains of victory so bright
And virtue spotless as a flower?
Who is this bravest knight?

> I am he, yea,
> I am he
> Who never spoke but right;
> Champion to heal mankind;
> To bring earth healing light!

But see, his robe is spattered red, his feet with crimson shod,
Like one stepped freshly from the press where grapes to pulp are trod.

> I bring the bread—
> From corn that grew beneath the Holy Rod;
> I bring the wine
> Of Sun-trod vine,
> In the chalice sipped by God.

VIA DOLOROSA

They tore the palms to strew his way,
   They tore down branches in ecstasy;
      And hearts are torn when we hear the cry
         Of 'Hosanna' torn to 'Crucify'.

They slept midst Gethsemane's olive-gnarled breath,
   They slept while he drank from the cup of death;
      And hearts are asleep to the trials of the day
         Till the trumpet blows life's blindness away.

They smote and scourged with birch and thong,
   They smote the right, set free the wrong;
      And hearts are smitten with blows of fate,
         And the trials of life that irritate.

They pressed the thorns into a ring,
   They pressed them down like crown on king;
      And hearts are pressed with scorn and spite,
         And the challenge of life to stand upright.

They nailed the wood midst the dust of the street,
   They nailed each hand, they nailed both feet;
      And hearts are nailed with distress and woe
         When burdens weigh down which life may bestow.

They rent his garments at the foot of the cross,
   There they lay rent on the foot-crushed moss;
      And hearts are weary—rent in twain—
         When darkness of life bears in in pain.

Filled with peace was the garden at dawn,
   Filled with joy of life reborn;
      Filled now are hearts, blessed from above,
         Wherein is risen the Lord of Love.

PATH TO A STAR

I dreamt of a tree in Eden
Whose rosy apples fair
Shone with dew of sunrise
With vine and corn
All newly born
And lark and linnet echoing there.

I dreamt of a tree in Eden
Whose apples, oh what plight,
Were devoured with eager gloating
By beasts of hell
As shadows fell
Chaining love and stinging sight.

I dreamt of a tree on Calvary
No apples did it bear
Among its boughs black-bending
But a thorn-crowned head
'Mongst roses red
A stream of life beyond compare.

I dreamt of a path half-hidden
To a tall tree leading far
In whose Heavenly branches
Shining bright
Immortal light
Like earth, through love, become a star.

NEW LIFE

The red resurrection of spring's green glory
Surges through the valley
Echoes in the air;
Dawn's new twittering, filled with feathered fancy
Melts winter languish
Lightens burden'd care.

The longing larches bristle with twigland's true tinsel
The front-gardened almond
Unveils her painted face
Stately cedars cleansed in the first spring sunshine
Blackthorn adance
In its blossom-white lace.

Red and orange heralds of spring's resurrection
Withies by the meadow
Where the current hastens free;
Christ in his Glory calls in his circling:
Death!
Stand forth!
Blind!
Turn and see!

MAYFAIR

Maypole's forest memories
Root-deep harvest heaven-gleaned
Chub-still waters dream-meandering:
Stirring with joy in the dawn of life's heralding.

Blossom-purple lilacs
Drooping-gold laburnam
Lawn-spread cherry-strewn foot-worn daisy-greenth:
Dawning with joy in the spring of life's burgeoning.

Costume—rainbow ribboned—
Breeze-fresh tantalised fluttering
Overcast sulkiness exiled resplendently:
Springing with joy in the wake of life's ecstasy.

Barber's pole, bright-woven
Plaited threads rotating
Festive frolickers gypsy-jigged intertwined:
Waking with joy in the dance of life's spiralling.

Bonds of friendship braided
Loved-ones guests and strangers
Colour-swathed spire, beyond death, heart-welcoming:
Dancing with joy in the depths of life's dignity.

MAY MORNING

All the egg-whisked lamb-frisk
Was white on the hill-side that morning.

Palm Sunday was a mere memory of shouts,
Hosannas that spilt from a watery sun
And spattered on the stones of Jerusalem's stone city;

Pentecost was a pending promise of white hope
Peeping from dove-white skies and flowering chestnuts:

But that morning
Was a day of white-frisked lamb-whisk,
Frothing on meadow and cloud,
On green and blue,
Tumbling from mother ewe and empty sepulchre,
Whisking from egg-white sun-dance,
Frisking from egg-gold sun-glow,
Fleece-fresh on the hill-side;

That May morning!

WHITE WHITSUN

White Whitsun's here with fields of hay;
The sun-filled clouds make glad the day,
While kek-stretching miles of smiling white
Cheer the dreary tarmac grey;
The chestnut's crowned in white array
And hedges dance with sprays of may;
    White Whitsun's here:
    Dark doubt away!

PERRYN ROUND

Not on the cobbles of the market square,
Not in the shadow of 'mother church',
    But in the great Perryn Round
    Beneath the blue of heaven,
      For three days of glory,
      The Cornishmen watched;
    Watched the gates of Heaven,
      Watched Hell's mouth,
        While above,
    In the great Cosmic round,
      The eye of Uriel
      The eye of Uriel
        Watched
      The future.

MIDSUMMER

Woven in the sun-touched tree-tops,
Cradled in the scattered pollen haze,
Glinting in the dew-pearled meadows,
    Nature lifts me towards the cosmic gaze:

Gaze which burns the soul with waiting,
Waiting till the sparkling spirits rise,
Rise in silver dance of summer glory,
    At the threshold of the warning skies.

DAWN'S DAY

Great sun of life!
From thy pharaonic throne
In midsummer heights,
Gazing with burning eye on deeds of men,
    Look down!
    And deign to tread the royal carpet of the skies
    Reddened with rich splendour
    Of atmosphere and light commingled.
        Descend, O descend!
        Hearken in the silence of impending night
        To the throb of folk, thronging round the fire
        Waiting with hushed breath and burning hearts
        Here on earth.

O great sun of love and life!
As the gremlins vanish ghost-like round the hills,
And as the languid lid of night their radiance dulls,
Grant this we pray;
    When, on the morrow, the new morn breaks,
    Rise in our hearts!
    Kindle there thy fire
    That we may know ourselves to be
    Children of the skies,
    Children of Dawn's Day.

2
Moving through corridors of time

DELPHI

Once, on the hill of Delphi,
          a wondrous sanctuary stood,
The sanctuary of Zeus' two sons,
          fed by the well-spring of good:

Surrounded by dancing maenads,
          Dionysus, high on the west,
The flowing folds of his robes
          by flowing crimson caressed;
While lit by the morning gold,
          in the eastern gable, aglow,
Apollo, encircled with muses,
          their blessings prepared to bestow.

And there by that sacred temple,
          the neophytes—masters in dream—
Delved into deepest mysteries,
          with flute-filled grace supreme;
And, beyond the inscribed pronaos,
          immortal lyrics were born,
While the oracle brought the people
          the voice of awakening dawn.

O, inspiring sun of Hellas!
          which shone through earth's dark night,
Shine on us, thy children,
          who seek again thy light:
Bless the vision splendid
          with inward-knowing bright,
And purify all ecstasy
          with heavenly, healing sight.

PROMETHEUS

From the peaks of Olympus Zeus threatens
                    in cloud-flashing anger he glowers
Glowers at the culprit now bound
                    by chains from Hephaestos' anvil.

    Prometheus pained on Caucasian peaks
    Dazed in the deluge of thundrous fury
    Yet spurred by the speech he inspired into men.

From the peaks of Olympus Zeus thunders
                    wrathful as storm-foaming ocean
While whirlwinds of rage he unleashes
                    on him who stood bold in his pathway.

    Prometheus flailed by the thundering wrath-roar
    Endlessly waiting; the anguish enduring
    Yet unrepentant in the teeth of the tribute.

From the peaks of Olympus Zeus rages
                    scowling dread torrents of anger
His bird of prey swooping downward
                    unrelentlessly pecking his victim.

    Prometheus mauled in mad-ferment of fury
    Wrenching chafe-chains as the vulture chisels
    Yet aflame with joy for the fire for Man.

THE CATACOMB OF PRISCILLA

From the depths of the ocean: the whale
From the depths of the whale: prophecy
From the depths of prophecy: a torch of light.

    Light in the heights of heaven
    Light in the circle of earth
    Light in the depths of the damned.

And in the lamp of the new-born heart: Light.
The light of Lazarus:

    Of death at the end of the road
    Of life standing forth reborn;
    Of hatred become love
    Of doubt become love
    Of love become giving;

    Heart-giving
    Deathless
    Hands uplifted.

RAVENNA

In the shimmering shifting sand,
In the shimmering grain of the desert dunes,
In the the grain-gritted wind of the pulverized plain,
With chipped-flint strength I scour.

In the furnace's fiery flare,
In the furnace's flux-flowing blinding flame,
Transmuted by its power.

In the sheen of reflected light,
In the sun-glanced glass-coloured garden of green
I unfold like rose in bower.

In mosaicist's skilful hands
In mosaicist's plaster-damp pattern-filled joy,
In Ravenna's twice-thirteen panels on high,
In Lazarus raised I flower.

In the sheep by the shepherd's hand,
In the sheep, where still waters of Paradise flow,
In the waters which soothe the Samaritan's soul,
In the fountain's freshness I shower.

In the cool of the arched arcades,
In the cool of the blue of the vaulting dome,
In the blue of the virgin's flowing robe,
I bathe in beauty's hour.

In basilica's cross of gold,
In basilica's marbled heaven-blessed walls,
In the heaven-blessed walls of the House of God,
Of God on earth, I tower.

RICHARD COEUR DE LION

Though Richard the Lionheart brave
Homeward bound from the Holy Land
In a secret tower like a slave
Was imprisoned by Leopold's scheming hand;

And though monarchs rejoiced at his fall
The hearts of his faithful were sad,
The minstrel, who once had played in his hall,
Journeyed forth to make him glad;

At the base of the castle grim,
He sang with anxious heart
While his eyes with tears were dim
From his lord so long to be forced apart;

Till, above, the melody clear
Came echoing sweet and bold;
And he knew he had found his king so dear
His king with crown of gold.

MAID OF ORLEANS

High-mounted on horse-back, the Maiden—
        The Maiden of France midst the cheering—
She rides with her company splendid—
        Midst banners, midst trumpets, midst lances.

Of humble-birth, circled by Nobles—
        By Nobles less noble than she is—
She rides in white armour triumphant—
        A marvel more wondrous than mermaid.

Her heart is afire with the angel—
        The angel who brought her God's message—
She rides towards honour and victory—
        Her countenance glowing like sunrise.

VOICES OF GOD

Thou Maid:

Born and bred by fertile, thriving vineyards,
 Sunny valleys, mills and hamlets nestling;
  Safe from wolf-prowled forest-shadows, evil,
   Far from armour-smitten, battle-stoking anvil;

   There, where peace and pasture, festal garlands,
   There, where well of healing, fairy laughter,
  There, where songs and dancing, gambols, picnics,
Thrill of skylarks fluttering in the ether-blue;

There, as gently as the flocks' soft nibbling,
 As magical as linden-blossom rustling,
  Yet certain as the very sword of Michaël,
   There thy Voices spoke of realms ineffable.

   That Maid, daughter of God:

From trembling awe her dauntless strength is wrested
 As she Heaven's call obeys from depths of soul,
  Turning from pastoral quietude and content
   To where the Fleur de Lis as battle ensign flies;

   Where once the mellow cadence of the shepherd's
   Pipe, lingered on the evening air,
  The hoof-snared drum-roll of charging cavalry now pounds
As the thronging company of lords she leads;

A country maid at home in kingly hall;
 Through her, nobility is ennobled,
  Royalty itself is consecrated;
   But nothing for herself she gains:

   For others all.

ROUND CAPE POINT

Wave upon wave
        Washing the shore
Atlantic's cold grey
        Indian blue.

Wave upon wave
        Midway the path
Nor founder nor fear
        When storm hunger growls.

Wave upon wave
        Buoyant with life
Joy in the deck-heave
        Cross brought to land.

LINES AS FROM DÜRER

Let those with valour sail the seven seas!
My canvas shall not feel the pluck of wind
But shall the briefest breath of spirit designate;
Reveal that spirit which with pluck for life,
Did find this earthly frame here fashioned
Craft enough; and the course of life
Banquet abundant for adventure's quickened hunger.

The course is set! This cap of white obeys
And yet's by black thoughts blinded, like rocky coast befogg'd;
This braid of white to its purpose truly holds
But the black weaves in and stealthily steers aside;
These sleeves of white willingly would come to grips
Did the stripes of black not lash the storms of hindrance
Into fury.

O captain of my soul!
Guide me, as my life's canvas spreads,
That my treasured cargo—shipped not from foreign shores,
But given freely, by a flowing heart—
Be not engulfed in stormy depths of soul;
But, like the Magi's gifts, safely brought
And laid at those same feet:
Of God my Saviour.

THE SIEGE OF LEYDEN 1574

High on the top of the tower
    Watchmen scouring dyke and polder
    Meat giving out
    Citizens brave
    Trust in comrades and in 'The Silent'
    Help on the way
    When the wind turns
    Gath'ring clouds will be scattered.

High on the top of the tower
    Watchmen plagued by thirst and hunger
    Bread running short
    Spaniards proud
    Dangling pardons—like cheese on mouse-trap
    Spurned with contempt
    'Firm to the death
    Freedom our right in religion.'

High on the top of the tower
    Watchmen's hope-starved hearts are weary
    Malt-cake is scarce
    Breach in the dykes
    Yet too low the tide to bear the convoy
    Till from the west
    Strikes the first gale
    Barges afloat through field and orchard
    Sea-beggars fierce
    Grapple with strength
    Townsfolk a bulwark defiant.

High on the top of the tower
    Watchmen keep face though famished and feeble
    Horse-flesh now gone
    Dogs and cats
    Slackened sails flap as again the wind veers
    Equinox lashing the desolate waters
    Besiegers besieged
    Panic their plight
    Black heaving waves ablaze in the darkness.

High on the top of the tower
    Watchmen mocked by the teeth of starvation
    Vermin consumed
    Waters devour
    Ramparts collapse with fear-striking thunder
    Then comes deliverance
    Night folds away
    Fleet bringing freedom is here.

FIDELIO

Dungeon is deep,
Jailer's face grave;
Lifeless he seems —
        Hopeless to save;

Yet in disguise,
Lantern in hand,
Bride ever brave
        As fortune has planned.

Defying the devil,
Though feeble and pained,
Never a flinch,
        Hardships disdained.

Watchman from tower,
Trumpet proclaims;
Tyrant's defeat;
        Evil in flames.

Prisoner awake;
No longer wait;
Relief is at hand—
        Welcome your fate.

GRACE DARLING

Silvery moon, soft in the sky;
Soft in the sky, diadem of stars;
Diadem of stars, glinting their light;
Bright constellations;
Star-sparkling splendour.

Fathoms below, lulled by the swell;
Lulled by the swell, bathed in the moon-white;
Bathed in the moon-white, surf-snoozing silver;
Travellers Ho!
Coast on their way.

Black-viced anvils
Frowning in the vault-void,
Glowering outriders
Of villainous storm-feast,
Obscuring night's glory
Blotting out planets
Mocking their orbiting;
Famished lightning
Flashing mastwards,
Teeth-gritted thunder-growling,
Death-hungry welkin
Hurling loose fury;
Luring heaving tonnage—
Tonnage tossed like matchwood—
Towards treacherous sand-banks;
Grist for breakers
Grinding maelstrom,
Rock-lurking ruggedness;
Jaws of the foam-lashed storm-monster gnashing.

Storm-blighted souls cry out for mercy;
Light-house holds firm in the onslaught perilous;
Keeper, roused by the cloud-capped thundering,
Bows to the bandersnatched burdenous buffeting—
Out to the rescue with fear-conquered heart-gold
Labouring, braving the wreck-wreaking elements.

THE LADY WITH THE LAMP

From the field of battle harsh the wounded come
From the cannon's deafening roar
From the charge of horses' hooves
    From thrust of lance
    From friends bereft
    With unstaunched wounds
In death's dark silence laid.

Through the corridors of peace she takes her lamp
Like an angel's light to them it seems
As she softly moves from bed to bed
    Her healing word
    Her soothing glance
    Her courage true
Each soul revives with life anew.

FLORENCE NIGHTINGALE
IN THE WINTER OF 1854/55

Not beside the roaring gun-wrath
Nor in face of flashing death-steel
Nor swept by flood of charging cavalry;
Hers no ruthless victory:

Hers the task of tireless service,
Fameless hours of pure devotion
By the beds of unknown soldiers
Nursing, wrestling, night-long watches—
Food of life for wounded, dying—
Fearless midst contagion.

With her lamp a saviour
In death's shadow shedding comfort
Through the ranks of blood-stained stretchers
Rank disease defying;

Calm she brings to pain-fraught features
Peace midst storm of battle-turmoil
Healing care to sword-slashed anguish
Grace and love to life-spent victory.

3
Striding through the land

ROSE HIPS

Rose-bud wake
Pink as dawn
Bright with dew
Beauty born.

Rose-bud open
Marvel rare
Made by God
Scenting air.

Rose-bud fade
Petals away
Hips grow red
Cheering the day.

CATKINS

Before the waiting buds unfold
By power of frost deterred,
Each hedge along the new-ploughed fields
A crop of cheery catkins yields
    Defying winter's cold.

No blizzard can their laughter drown—
Let it blow from north or east;
Matching the lichen on cottage rooves
Their mustardy livery dustily moves
    Next winter's thorny crown.

And so, when life would claw like thorn,
May the cloak of love protect;
And when night's threatening shadows thrust
May the pollen, of my heart's-joy dust
    With gold the coming morn.

WINTER IN ST JAMES'S PARK

When the sinking sun in the darkening sky
               sings its wintry evensong,
  And the glove-puppet clouds
  With dove-grey breast
     Sail towards the gleaming west;

When the bud-tight rose on its stilt of thorn
               bravely uncurls in the frost-edged air,
  And the tapestry of turquoise
  On the stream, ice-cold
     Is undershot with ripples of gold;

When the criss-cross branches and trunks of the trees
               bristle and jostle and jangle aloft,
  And the homing birds
  On lonely wing
     Plaintively in the silence sing:

  My strengthening soul brings warmth and light
  Like a field of gold in the melting night.

NORTHERN LIGHTS

When night descends, descends on drowsy day,
And stars of twilight blink in heaven's depths,
A shimmering cross arises in the darkness,
In widening veils of majesty and light,
Like wakening choirs of quivering harps in silence—
The silence of the sky, the shimmering voice of night.

That light-filled curtain hovering in the heavens
Reminds us of a mystery now gone
When star on star, in mighty constellation
Was more than light—an image of great power,
Fertile in the wide imagination
Of an earlier age, still dreaming in God's bower.

SPRING SHOWERS

When the clouds drop their showers in spring
And swallows swoop on the wing
    With brooks at play
    As they splash on their way
And mountain lambs to their dams still cling;

When the river which winds through the plain
Brims its banks, so firm, with the rain
    And cattle are seen
    Neath poplars green
And buttercups golden open again;

When beech woods break into song
With morning's dawn-filled throng
    And winter's blast
    Is spent and past
As the play of light is bright and long;

When each bush with blossom is dressed
And the blackbird peeps from her nest
    And still the storm
    As earth grows warm:
The life in my heart grows brave and blest.

BLACKBIRD IN SPRING

She builds her nest with twig and branch
    'Mongst April bloom,
And weaves it deftly with her beak
    Like weft on loom;

'Neath skies of blue at warbling dawn
    She lines her bower
Soft with moss and down—while tucked below
    The violets flower.

Her speckled eggs hatch one by one
    Beneath her breast;
She spreads her wings and keeps her chicks
    Against them pressed;

Then from the bush, her nest brim-full,
    She flies for food:
Beak-bulged she hops to fill the mouths
    Of her small brood.

SHEEP BELL

When shepherds in spring-shine sun are a-piping,
Their new-born lambs at their side,
> Their laughter so merry,
> Their cheeks red as cherry,
As they dance for joy in the pastures pied.

When shepherds in summer their flocks are a-folding,
Beneath the fair-blue sky,
> Their hearts all smiling,
> While their fleeces are piling,
As, with sleeves rolled up, their shears they ply.

When shepherds in evening light are a-resting
And sun is setting gold,
> A toothful tasty
> Of home-cooked pastry,
As they thank the good Lord for life on the wold.

When shepherd at night hears the angels a-singing
Their song in his soul so mild;
> In his dreaming arm,
> A lamb so calm,
And sheep-bell for the Holy Child.

POISED AT HIS EYRIE

The mountain torrent
Has no time to wait
Splashing o'er boulders
In fullest spate.

In shimmering speed
It cascades on its way
In precipitous plunging
And clouds of spray.

While above each peak
Of rock and snow,
Watching in silence
The turmoil below,

The eagle dwells—
In such heights at ease—
With strength-spread wings
And eye that *sees*.

IN THE COUNTY OF SUSSEX

Where the seagulls swerve and sway on cloud-white wing
O'er the steep sharp cliffs o' th' Sussex shore;

Where the sun-dappled deer drift with delicate tread
Across bracken-bathed brows o' th' Sussex hills;

Where the trembling mice scamper empty away
'Neath the stiff standing staddle-stones on Sussex farms;

Where the huntsman's horn alerts the hart and hind
'Midst dense cool depths o' th' Sussex woods;

Where the nimble lambs bleat each bounteous spring
On the steep tufty turf o' th' Sussex downs;

Where the pibald pony plods patiently with his pack
Among the wet windy ways o' th' Sussex Weald;

Where the close cropped clover by cattle is grazed
In the mist-moist meadows o' th' Sussex clay:

There—Man, with his home and farm and trade
Cares for the creatures the Creator hath made.

ALPINE COWHERD

Like a crown brimmed with jewels, the peaks glow in ethereal skies,
Hailing the day!
O'er the thrill of the air, and the chill of the bilberry dew
Dimpling clouds drift;
Waters ripple and trill as they spill in their sparkling cascades—
Playful and swift;
While the harebells a-dangle give welcome to butterfly flight
In the sun's dappled ray.

The precipitous scramble-screed crags are the chamois' home—
Freely they stray;
    In the cool of the shadow-pooled slopes where snow lies soft—
Quietly they rest;
    Or through rock-echoing rumble of flashing storms they roam—
Calm, undistressed;
    In God's hand they stand neath a temple of stars; all fears
He will allay.

    While below in the field-quilted valley, the cowherd bends
Bundling the hay;
    His sickle and shovel and stool and simple tools,
Inside the stall;
    As hoof-deep in stubble, in the bowl of the hills, the cattle
Wait for his call;
    Till the tingle of bells to all within ear-shot tells
His voice they obey.

How old, heaven knows, his leather hose and hat-feather
Jaunty as jay;
    His hazel-wand droops idle in his hand,
Peaceful the cattle go
    With gentle amble and udders creamy-deep,
Mellow they low;
    As bumble-bees mumble, they browse past fennel sweet
Upon their way.

    For a moment, at the fresh-filled water trough,
Thirsty they stay;
    Then follows the mangold-wurzle-crunch in the gloom,
Gladdening his heart;
    He marvels at the world—and thinks of home,
In summer, apart,
    While them a milking song he soothing lulls,—
And marvel he well may.

PINE GRIPPING GRANITE

Rage torrents and break
            in glad thundering, down on the rocks;
Lash spray! Swirl foam!
      They rejoice at your shattering shocks.

Blaze, sun in the sky!
            Bake the conifer-carpel-scales loose;
Wake spiralling dreams
      from your pin-cushioned pillows of spruce.

Laugh evergreen heart
            as your flakes feel the flap of the wind;
Quake not at the blast
      when the fear-flooded forest is dinned.

Plucked boldly aloft,
            bid farewell to the whorls of thy birth;
Dance ovule in hope
      in the vortices' heaven-filled mirth.

Light down on thy ledge
            when the storm is lulled to rest;
Labour for thy life!
      Rope-rooted, thou art blessed.

Deep-creviced strength!
            No rock too hard to crack;
Ice-bounded slopes!
      No joy shalt thou lack.

SCHAFFHAUSEN

Supported still by parent peaks,
I tread the descent from my noble birth—
My childhood rills neath the starry heavens,
       Tumbling with song in the mountain's mirth.

Through fairy-tale forest-filled bride-white beauty,
Sun-flooded gold-leafed branches each morn;
The gentians in spring in the dancing meadows,
       Dewed in the thrill-throated throb of the dawn.

Cool as the ferns in the red-resined pine-woods,
I bathe in the wonder of sun on the lake,
Lapping through the dream-long drowsy summer.
       Till my course to the falls bids me courage take.

With clarion call they welcome my coming,
In uproar a-plunge as they bid me spate;
Unmitigated turmoil, full-tilt, cascading,
       With bated breath, I fulfill my fate.

Beneath sky, down-driven by the Gods, I pay
The joy-rigidifying turbine's toll;
New-limbed, star-frenzied, full-purposed, I seek
       To gather the shreds of my shattered soul.

In seven-leagued boots, I'll join earth's traffic,
Striding twixt massifs of schist and the like,
While, remembering the blue in my swirl-soiled waters,
       Pass farm and factory, trout and pike.

In full career I'll plough through the gorge,
Its vineyards terraced for good or ill,
With guaranteed summer thaw-freed waters
       And winter rains warm from vale and hill.

And when my ice-jammed fog-jogged journey
In the ebb of the year will caution claim,
I'll strive for wisdom to show the way onward
       That, when life is done, there will be no shame.

SERTSEY

Swirl of fire
Billowing smoke

Lava spills
Churning the foam

Slaking steam
Wave-shaken scarps

Fire is tamed
Island's new birth.

TEAK

Swoon—sweltering heat of day
Beneath burning blue;
Strain-chained the harnessed beasts
Trustful and true.

Teak-giants forest felled
Logs huge in length,
Hauled down the mountain clefts
Vital with strength.

DISCOVERY

Through the hot and humid swamp-gloom
Night follows day
Day follows night
Inky waters darkly snaking
Gliding, rippling, wending wearily
Day follows night
Night follows day
Rapids riding, explorers revelling
On their tortuous way.

Through the green exuberance tunnelling
Steam through the rain
Rain through the steam
Savage thorns, festoon-flowered buttresses
Dangling tendrils, deep dense undergrowth
Rain through the steam
Steam through the rain
Through the matted thicket penetrating
Goal they will attain.

From the listless silence emanating
Deep in the wild
Wild in the deep
Glub-tubbed hippos, snap-jawed crocodiles
Jungle of gutterals, screechings, jabberings
Wild in the deep
Deep in the wild
Fearless forging, hope unsuffocated
Scarred but not defiled.

Safe past the brink of lethal waterfalls
Guides them God's hand
God's hand them guides
Safe from malaria, ambush, leopard-spring
Poisonous barbs of teeth-filed cannibals
God's hand them guides
Guides them God's hand
In peace, in fragrance, towering palm-shade
Charted the new land.

SUNSET OVER THE PAMPAS

Ocean-red the quavering grassland.
Close-cropped clover, luxuriant thistles,
Rich alfalfa, fodder fattening,
Flaxen spears of nodding pampas—
Fleecy-rose plumes in the blush of the sunset.

    Best beef cattle beside the wind-break,
    Grazing short-horns, Aberdeen Angus,
    Pedigree Herefords, herded by the water-tank,
    Born and bred in the path of the Pampero,
    Tussock-raised stock of the silt-sandy loess.

        Maté brewed by the sun-baked adobe,
        Rock-a-bye baby in the roof-dangled bullock-hide,
        Twang of guitar in the grass-woven whispering.

            Tale-telling poncho-clad estanchio-proud gauchos,
            Bare-backed tales of lasso-conquered cattle-leagues,
            Galloping thrills of the hoof-hobbling bolas.

    Masters of beast
    Of stiletto
    Of Self.

AUTUMN SUNRISE OVER THE ORWELL

    Inland:
    A scraggy scrawg of rooks
    Whirled untidily over the rusting sycamores
    Into a noisy cloud
    Which cracked the egg-shell smoothness of dawn
    Stirring beyond the estuary.

Tide was out:
A mill-pond stilness
Waded silently over the mud-banks
And over the salt-marshes
With mist
Lingering like lost sheep
And the odd wader
Preening importantly
On a Persian carpet of light-filled ooze
Standing bemused
As if overlooked by the weather forecaster.

While the tide of sunrise
Washed
Washed from the east
In waves of jewelled light.

And the silver hush of the sky:
Crescendoed
Into a cornucopia of morning radiance
Gliding full-sailed into every creak
Rolling among the low hills in fertile joy
Drooping mountainously over the gull-dappled plain
Hurdling like athlete over the undulations of birch and willow,
   furrow and stubble
Greening the fresh beards of sprouting winter wheat
   and the jaunty moustaches of weed upon the ploughed fields
Resting in quiet pools, like lining in a nest,
Glinting in the breeze-shimmered aspens
Breathing into the gnat-clouds of songsters skylarking overhead
Faithfully etching the swan-twined streams and ditches
   and their sentinelled banks of poplars
    whose foliage was moulting in the drifting autumn air,
Dazzling the very mirror of the mind
Fanning the very heart of hope
Echoing with new-created splendour
The long-once-voiced …
  And
  There
  Was
  Light.

4
The flow of manhood

FLOW OF MANHOOD

Silent sands lie waiting
While the tide is turning;
Spreading foam like drifts of snow
Day and night through ebb and flow;
While the tide is turning
Silent sands lie waiting.

Silent sands leap wave-borne
In the surge-strong tide-joy;
Brave, unbridled, horse-white breakers
Echoing dance of Gods, their makers;
In the surge-strong tide-joy
Silent sands leap wave-borne.

Silent sands lie star-washed
Bereft of life, yet life-blessed;
Rippled runnelled, through timeless motion
Finger-prints of earth's great ocean:
Bereft of life, yet life-blessed
Silent sands lie star-washed.

Tide of fate is waiting
For the flow of Manhood;
Ear on shell for heaven's stars' choiring
Strength of heart for life-inspiring:
As the flow of Manhood
Tide of fate is turning.

SAVED FROM THE STORM

Sail in the wildness of storm
Drifting like gull without hope
Buffeted, beaten and bruised by the gale
Which tears it to shreds, snapping rope:

Sail in the wildness of life
Longing for stilness and rest,
Reach for the hands holding hope for thee,
Like gull on the cliff by its nest.

SALMON

In the silvery waters
The silver salmon leap
As they dart on their silvery way
With their glittering scales
They leap over falls
In pure mountain streams at play;

But when the sun
In heaven high
Calls them back to the ocean blue
They return with joy
Through shady pools
To start their life anew.

SEALS

Basking in the Arctic sunshine
Fields of snow and ice their homelands
Dozing on their rocky ledges
Bloated floaters' flap-flopped flippers
Schools of seals together huddled
Till their hunger calls them seawards
Stirring the slumber-blubbered creatures;

Slithering down to waters welcoming
Diving in glee midst the fish-silvered oceans
Shoals inter-darting neath teeth-crunching ice-floes.

FISH

In Neptune's
Green waters
Shoal twining
Swift gliding;

Now darting
Now diving
In caves of
The ocean:

Now rising
Tails lashing
Waves splashing
Fins feath'ring;

Tide swelling
Foam frothing
Fish glinting
In sunlight.

THE OARSMAN'S SONG

O sailor the oars now grasp
    Grasp them with strong hands
Hands to row through the current keen
    Keen to the shores of my kinsman's lands.

My kinsman's lands are bleak
    Bleak for lack of work
Work I bring with strength of heart
    Heart and hand—no task I'll shirk.

THE LIGHT-HOUSE ·

From the calm of the coast-guard's
        cliff-poised cottage,
Neath heaven's highway,
        paved with stars and planets,
Bright beam,
        breaking the brooding darkness,
Warning wary mariners
        of wave-washed rock-teeth;
Or when perilous peals
        of thunder threaten,
And drowning deluge
        devours the dazed deck-hands:
All would be lost,
        failing loyal light-house,
Saving ship's sailors
        from snatching storm-snarl.

FISHERFOLK

Golden glow at heaven's sun-filled gateway
Shining o'er the ships and shimmering waters;
Smoke from cottage chimneys, cheek by jowl
Coils, curls, while flocks of gulls come screaming;
Till to work the townsfolk come a-tumbling
Women, shawls on shoulders—men in sea-boots;
Fair or foul, they face each day's new challenge
With willing hearts and hands to help each other.

ANCHOR

Clouds clash:
 anvils overhead in frown-fraught thundering;

Sea heaves:
 waters waging war in lashing spite;

Spray smites:
 cliff tops drenched in rivulets' wild foaming;

Salt stings:
 sailors hauling ropes in dreadful plight;

Rock deep:
 anchor holding firm the heaving vessel;

Waves pound:
 shuddering hull and deck in maddening glee;

Fear gulps:
 deluge pounding crew like grinding sandstone;

Hope wins:
 storm is past and life once more breathes free.

VIKING FIGURE-HEAD

Strong the long boat's gust-gutted timbers
Wild the welkins wind-wailed fury
Throat-raged thunder's Thor-flung challenge.

Strong the figure-head's gilt-glad gliding
Blade-straight through the blast-boiled buffeting
Prow-prized prince, like ship's proud promontary.

Strong the sailors's strife-strained squall-struggle
Rope-hauling sinews, salt-smitten sea-lords;
Scorn on land-lubbers' limp-laggard laziness.

Strong the folk-filled harbour, bulwark-bold
Greeting the gale-gruelled galleon's cargo
While figure-head unflustered rides victoriously.

MIMIR'S WELL

Eye of wisdom,
Sound of peace;
By weaving waters, waters whispering;
In magic mood
Of Mimir's well
From grip of evil bring release.

Eye of wisdom,
Sound of peace;
In Magic mood of Mimir's well,
Sacrificed
For sins of men,
God's gifts of goodness never cease.

FASHIONING THOR'S HAMMER

Though the gnat
  Bit and buzzed
While the bellows
  He clenched;
Though his eyes
  With the pain
Were blinded
  And drenched;

Though the flare
  From the forge
Frizzed the hair
  On his head;
Though the clang
  Of the hammering
Filled him
  With dread:

He clung to his mission,
He gripped unafraid;
He clung and he clutched
Till the hammer was made.

THE SLAYING OF FAFNIR

Great dearth of trees and flowers prevailed;
Scorched earth on either hand assailed;
Sword blessed by Odin in his hand he held;
Courage of lion in his arm up-swelled;
Fervour of sun in his heart there burned
As glittering worm uncurled and churned.

Forth flashed the steel,
Trusty and true;
Birds' song he heard,
And their voices he knew.

SWORD OF SIGURD

The smith took the shards of the king's sturdy weapon,
And blew up the fire to a bright dazzling flare;
The youth stood astounded as the sparks sped around him,
His eyes glowing bright in the red of the glare;

While blow upon blow smote the smith on the anvil,
His hammer he hurled with a deftness unknown;
Until, when the shards he had welded together,
The sword bore the strength of a God on his throne.

GRANI

With a whinny
With a neigh
With a swish of his tail
He speeds o'er turf and stone;

While he pounds
On the ground
With a thundering sound
He gallops all alone.

The sparks
Shower around
Like cymbals at dawn
As the flints clash under each shoe;

Till with jubilant joy
He swerves to the boy

His master,
Faithful,
True.

BREAKING IN

Mane and forelock,
Hooves well shod;
Plod or gallop,
Track well trod.

Tight-strapped saddle,
Stirrup, spur;
Bit and bridle,
Pennon, fleur.

Burnished armour,
Well-gripped lance;
Knight and squire,
Fate or chance.

Faithful stallion,
Rein obey,
Rider mounted:
Face the fray.

GRAIN GROWING

Flame burn:
Blacksmith's fire;
Cling, Clang!
Blacksmith's beat;
Bend, curve:
Shoe of iron;
Nails firm:
Horse's feet.

Heave, Ho!
Plough the field;
Shine Sun;
Grow the grain;
Brown flour:
Mix and bake;
Bread for all:
Grace again.

THE PLOUGHMAN

He hears the wind a-blowing,
A-blowing through the gorse;
While bending o'er the furrows,
He gently guides his horse.

He hears the wind a-whisp'ring,
A-whisp'ring in his ear;
While bending o'er the furrows,
His way dispels all fear.

He hears the wind a-sighing,
A-sighing in his heart;
While bending o'er the furrows,
He keeps them straight, apart.

He hears the wind a-buffeting,
A-buffeting his back;
While bending o'er the furrows,
He holds the plough in track.

He hears the wind a-fading,
By evening peace carressed;
And ponders at his fireside
The tides of fate so blessed.

BEOWULF

Bowel of blackness Beowulf braved;
Foul the fumes that filled the air;
Dismal darkness drenched with death—
Woke the hero's steel-strong will:
Grendel grim he, grappling, slew;
Voice of victory fanned his fame.

JACOB'S LADDER

Head-rest and foot-stool:
    the earth;
Voices of angels
    and wings,
Greeting in chorus
Jacob the Dreamer:
Priests with their candles
And crown-headed Kings.

Ladder descending
    from heaven;
Flourish of light
    and love,
Greeting in chorus
Jacob awakening:
Strength below
For strength above.

NOAH'S ARK

In the wind, o'er the waves, dove's wing
To brave Noah, olive branch bring;
With the animals, floats the ark
With its souls—God-saved from dark
To Light, to Life, to Love, to Land;
For Heaven and Earth are Rainbow-spanned.

DAVID'S SLING

Fierce Goliath of giant fame
Faces David's brave-bright flame;

David, sling in hand, doth wait;
He trusts in God to guard his fate;

Goliath shouts and shakes his spear;
In David's heart awakes no fear;

Strong Goliath strikes in vain:
With slender sling the giant is slain.

5
Poems for morning and evening

HIGH IN THE SKY

High in the sky the shining sun
Firm in earth the growing tree;
We saw the logs and pile them up,
And light the fire the flames to see;
Curling, twirling, burning, yearning—
Fiery flare a-dance with glee—
Like the sunlight, to be free;
Sun and flames with warmth are kindling
Fire of my own—at rest in me.

STREAM EVER FLOWING

Stream ever flowing,
Life giving sun;
Love in my heart,
Day has begun.

Stream ever flowing,
O'er stones on its way;
Strength in my limbs,
To help where I may.

Stream ever flowing,
Star-filled the sky;
Light in my mind,
Open mine eye.

CIRCLING SUN

Circling sun
In heaven blue;
Shining strength
Within my heart:

Hands I lift
To thee in joy,
Day in window,
Open door:

On path of life
I make my way,
Meet my friends
And greet the day.

THE HARVEST OF THE JOURNEY

Not the mileage of the journey
Cut and dried and Roman-straight;
But the harvest of the winding road—
Fresh with granite-clear air
Cool with lime-welling springs
Rich with the gold of each traveller
Shining in the joy of all.
Not the mileage of the clock
But the harvest of the winding road:
This is life's journey.

THE SUN OF HEAVEN SHINES ABOVE ME

The sun of heaven shines above me—
Sail my thoughts from star to land.

The cloak of heaven folds around me—
Warm my heart and full my hand.

The strength of heaven streams right through me—
Firm my feet on earth to stand.

WEAVING NIGHT'S THREADS
INTO DAY

Along the moonlight's pathway
With silver steps I tread
Wending above the mountain's height
Wending above the clouds of white
        The Heavens o'er my head.

Through doors of time I wander
Through doors that no time mars
Following the angel of my birth
Following the angel, friend of earth
        On ways as old as stars.

And when the night is ended
And morning has begun
I weave the thread of day new-bright
Into the pattern of the night
        As garment for the sun.

THE PEACE OF NIGHT

Owl on the wing in the twilight
Stars in the winking heaven
Crescent the moon soft-golden
Like sail on cloud-boat drifting.

Angels on wing around me
Singing uplifting, guiding
Bestowing calm strength for living,
And filling the night with peace.

WHEN AT NIGHT

When at night in the starry turning heavens
    My soul is at repose
    Then pathways bright
    Lead to the light
Of the land where the wind of the spirit blows.

When dark skies of grey eclipse the sun
    Of childhood's radiant days
    That light I bear
    With cherished care
Down the paths where earth-found friendship plays.

When the planets circling on their way
    Cause friendship's paths to part
    That spirit sun
    Of true love spun
With steadfast trust shines in my heart.

THE RIVER OF SLEEP

At eve on the river of sleep
I ferry my boat towards heaven
Past shimmering fishers of light
To the shores of the ocean of starland.

Soft winds of joy fill my sails
And blow plumes of foam around me,
While angels with blissful harps
And jubilant songs bid me welcome.

They brim my bowl with strength,
Fill the folds of my cloak with beauty,
And pave my way with peace,
With the peace and calm of their voices.

IN MY LIMBS EARTH'S STRENGTH

In my limbs earth's strength is stirring:
Rocks and meadows, ocean free
Gentle rainfall, trees so stately
Breezes blowing full of glee;
In my limbs earth's strength is stirring.

In my heart the sun is streaming:
Light supreme within my soul
Fills my life with golden glory
Guides me nearer to my goal;
In my heart the sun is streaming.

In my mind the stars are shining:
Shining with a light serene,
Like a jewelled crown they gather
In my mind as radiant queen;
In my mind the stars are shining.

In the night my angels call me
From the realms of star and sun;
Ris'n from sleep, new joy I carry
As strength within till day is done.

GUARDIAN ANGEL

Guardian angel, watch me
Guardian angel strong
Watch me as I wend my way
Though the way be long.

Guardian angel, bear me
Guardian angel bright
Bear me through the land of sleep
Through the starry night.

Guardian angel, guide me
Guardian angel stern
Guide me though the path be steep
Be with me when I learn.

Guardian angel, bless me,
Angel full of love
Bless me as I heark to Thee
In God's realm above.

A NIGHT SONG

Trees stretching stately,
Starred by the night;
　　　　Stately stretching trees,
　　　　Towering in might.

Wind blowing softly
Stir without cease;
　　　　Softly blowing wind,
　　　　Spirit of peace.

Moon glowing quietly,
Silver her beam;
　　　　Quietly glowing moon,
　　　　Pathway to dream.

SUN OF LIGHT

Sun of Light:
> Shine in my heart
> When day has begun;
In my heart shine
> O Light of Sun.

Rose of Joy:
> Flower in my heart
> Where life's thorn grows;
In my heart flower
> O Joy of Rose.

Crown of Stars:
> Robed in my heart
> When sleep wafts down;
In my heart robed
> O Starry Crown.

Choir of Angels:
> Sing in my heart
> Through night's clouded fire;
In my heart sing
> O Angel Choir.

Gold of Earth:
> Love in my heart
> Where life's ways unfold;
In my heart love
> O Earth of Gold.

Notes
(for teachers and parents)

Each poem is listed in the notes in the order in which it appears in the book. The number following each poem indicates the page on which the poem appears. Where there is more than one poem on a page the poem that appears first on the page is listed first. So, for example, there are two poems on page 3. The first one is 'Michaelmas song' (3a) and the second one is 'Bridge building' (3b).

Watching the year—festivals and seasons

Meteor showers and us (2)
Michaelmas song (3a)
Bridge building (3b)

The festival of Michaelmas is the first festival of the academic year:

(2) It is heralded in the summer months by showers of shooting stars often in the region of Taurus. This meteoric iron, rushing into earth's atmosphere, serves as a reminder of the iron content of the human blood.

(3a) At this time of year, it is not only the academic world that makes a new beginning. In an earlier age, ploughmen traditionally changed jobs at Michaelmas, often sealing the agreement they made with their new master with a hand-shake, rather than a contract in the modern sense. Presiding over this festival season is Libra, the zodiacal image of Man's struggle to maintain a balance in his inner life. This has been expressed down the ages in several ways—the overcoming of the dragon being the one most familiar in European culture.

(3b) Through the human conquest of technological power, iron has been put to uses in recent centuries that were formerly unthinkable. The right handling of such power depends on human morality retaining the upper hand. This is perhaps one way of seeing the Michaelmas theme in the modern setting. In verse three, the pronunciation of the fourth word in each line requires three syllables: Micha-el (cf. Raphael).

Harvest Loaf (4a)
Although Michaelmas and harvest in temperate climates are in close proximity, the two festivals can easily be celebrated separately. This verse might well serve as a harvest grace. It should gently emphasise the anapaestic rhythm wherever it occurs, for example at the beginning: *Fields of corn* (vv—).

St Martin (4b)

This saint was a popular figure in the Middle Ages, as is witnessed by the many different forms in which he appears in stained glass, illuminated manuscripts and so on. Even as late as El Greco an impressive rendering of that moment in Martin's biography is depicted where he is dividing his cloak for the beggar. This short verse—one would not, perhaps, wish to linger a great deal over the festival—is written in iambic pentameter, thus giving an approach to it through a rhythm more suited to the Middle School.

Arum et Rosa (5)

Of all plants that carry with them important symbolism, the lily and rose are possibly the most ubiquitous. Delicacy, restraint and purity are some of the qualities associated with the former—in popular image it was the flower traditionally held by Gabriel at the annunciation. Whereas the latter, despite its exquisite beauty, has a certain robustness and potential to proliferate. Its victory over the thorns is also a telling and strongly suggestive image.

Good tidings at Yule (6)

The winter solstice occasions remarkable festival experiences in many different cultural settings, the most profound, in some ways, being that of the re-birth of the sun itself. This comes clearly across the ages from the ruggedly vigorous celebrations of the Vikings, many elements of which have been taken into the modern Christmas. But not all: some of these appear in this poem, such as the gathering of the mistletoe by the priests by spreading out a white cloth beneath the tree where it grew; the central importance of the boar's head, as part of the feast, we find echoed in the traditional and often rowdily sung carol 'The Boar's Head as I Understand'; the huge yule log itself was a sacred emblem, surrounded with rites when being brought in—as here briefly outlined—and regarded as being precious for its healing properties in its final form of burnt ash.

Three mothers (7)

Each soul feels a relationship to the first two of these: Nature (or Natura, which term helps to lift the concept of outer nature towards something more vibrant with 'being'), and Eva, the original ancestor. The 'Madonna' may be seen as a transformation of both or either of these.

The Donkey's Journey (8)

The sound 'D' is a continuous feature of this poem, each line being unobtrusively concluded with it. It is modulated, verse by verse, by a seven-fold sequence of vowels: phonetically they are o, a (ah), 'I', ee, ay, u, au—a linguistic journey in itself.

Three Kings (9)

One aspect of the festival of Epiphany is that of *manifestation*. This comes to rhythmic expression in the poem through the more inward trochee (−v) being superceded by the more animated dactyl (−vv).

St Bride of Iona (10)
William Sharp, in his penetrating portrait of St Bride, places much emphasis on the various journeys that form an integral part of the legend. That these journeys have inner significance is suggested in this poem by the reflective nature—reflective as far as material is concerned—of the two shorter lines following each long one.

Dawn Chorus (11)
As a juggler tosses his juggling rings, or whatever, from hand to hand, this poem moves to and fro, with increasing buoyancy, through some of the phenomena of early spring.

Pass Over (12)
Death and Resurrection form the uniting factor in the three images here alluded to. The autumn tree arouses in the soul the contra-forces to what is taking place in the Fall externally in the world. Turner's well-known and dramatic *Cottage destroyed by an avalanche* (in the Grimsons), painted in 1810, calls for mighty human forces to pit themselves against the positively destructive powers of nature. The altar-piece at Colmar, painted by Grünewald brings touches of realism to the very peak of poignancy, not only in the physiognomy of its figures but also in the gesture of the hands.

Joseph of Arimathea (13)
Traditionally, on account of his services to Rome, Joseph of Arimathea gained permission from Pontius Pilate to take the body of Jesus of Nazareth down from the cross and place it in the sepulchre. His own subsequent imprisonment and remarkable liberation, his associations with the grail cup and his journey to and connection with Glastonbury all go to make him an enigmatic yet important figure.

The knight stained from battle (14)
The rousing clarion that sounds through the opening verses of Isaiah 63 inspired William Herebert in the 14th century to express thoughts and sentiments such as are contained in this poem, here presented in dialogue form.

Via Dolorosa (15)
Such images and inner situations as are here described are only suitable for older classes, presupposing a certain degree of maturity of soul. It has not been the intention to follow the exact 'stations of the cross', though the mood and handling of the subject may be seen as a transformation of such a 'way'.

Path to a star (16)

The tree of knowledge, so-called, bears two moods, sharply contrasted in that they reflect the human situation *before* the eating of the apple and *after*. Reference to the 'tree' of Calvary links to the legend that connects the wood of the two trees. The third tree, may be thought of as rising above the physical into the sphere of resurrection, typified by artists from the time of the early catacombs onward. Indeed, the motif of uplifted hands derives from even earlier civilisations—as the 'orantes' gesture.

New Life (17a)

These images, of larch, of blackthorn and of the withies lining the stream—maybe dogwood, too—mingled with the twittering of birds, emphasise how nature follows the festival mood in spring (in contrast to the situation in autumn).

Mayfair (17b)

The gradual dominance of the dactyl (—vv) over the trochee (—v) is an important rhythmic feature of this poem, conveying the mood of lively dance. The reference to the barber's pole, is merely to the red and white spiral with which the pole is/was striped as often as not.

May Morning (18)
White Whitsun (19a)

Just as black is traditionally the colour of mourning, so white carries with it a mood of spirit-bathed joy. These two poems reveal different facets of this, the first being couched in a style more accessible, perhaps, to the adolescent, the second referring directly to *Whit*sun itself. Kek, referred to in *kek-stretching miles*, is a local Warwickshire name for cow parsley (*Anthriscus sylvestris*) which is found growing in the hedgerows from April onwards.

Perryn Round (19b)
Midsummer (20a)
Dawn's day (20b)

These three poems are concerned with the festival connected with the summer solstice. 'The Perryn Round' (19b) was where the Cornish Mystery Plays were performed, significantly, out in the open. Of the archangels, Uriel is the one who traditionally presides at this time of year. A more inward, lyrical approach to the festival is encapsulated in 'Midsummer' (20a), while 'Dawn's Day' (20b) explores in declamatory style the supremacy of the sun's regency at this time. At the same time, the special quality of midsummer eve/night, so close to the hearts of peoples in the far north with their all-night midsummer fires, provides equally important associations.

Moving through corridors of time

Delphi (22)
Hexameter is not a metrical favourite with English-speaking poets as it is a rhythm depending very much on length rather than on stress. It may prove effective if this poem is recited in such a way that the vowel sequences slightly predominate.

Prometheus (23)
This poem was written for a combined group of 10 and 11 year-olds. The older pupils were principally involved with the hexameters (vv.1, 3 & 5), the younger group with the alliterative verses (2, 4 & 6).

The Catacomb of Priscilla (24)
At Via Salaria Nuova 430, in Rome, this catacomb may be visited. The mood of the poem springs from the images of Jonah and Lazarus that remain there.

Ravenna (25)
In AD 493 Theodoric led his Ostrogoths as conquerors to the region of Italy where Ravenna now stands. This poem explores some of the manufacturing aspects of the mosaics, associated with Ravenna, as well as the images that arose at the hands of the artists.

Richard Coeur de Lion (26a)
Maid of Orleans (26b)
Voices of God (27)
These three poems are examples of how important it is for history to be taught to the pre-adolescent largely through the deeds of great personalities. Occasionally these border on the legendary; this bears witness to the fact that an earlier consciousness also saw the stage of world events in a similar light.

Round Cape Point (28)
The mood of discovery is one to which every youngster at some point responds with enthusiasm. Such a poem might give children of this age ideas for expressing—other than in prose form—their own impressions of the life that explorers led and endured.

Lines as from Dürer (29)
The content of this poem is very specific. It refers to Dürer's self-portrait of 1498, painted when he was 26 and shortly after he had created his anagram. That he wanted to be thought of as modern can be seen in his elegant, fashionable clothes. On the other hand, it is the same year in which he produced his woodcuts, *Secret Revelation of St John*. These alone, ensured his immediate fame throughout Europe. The self-portrait is oil on wood and now hangs in the Prado, Madrid.

The Siege of Leyden, 1574 (30)
A turning point in the history of the Netherlands was when the Dutch
were able to reverse the effects of the Siege of Leyden by the Spanish
forces of occupation in 1574. In some ways this was the brightest feather
in the cap of their hero and leader William the Silent. One way in which
the mood is obtained in this poem is through the listless short lines
interspersed with the otherwise tidal flow of the longer lines. This
contrast can be used subtly to build up towards the climax in the last
verse.

Fidelio (31)
This noble theme was chosen by Beethoven for his only opera
(produced 1805). The setting is 15th century Spain. A certain forceful-
ness is gained in the poem through the almost unflinching use of the
rhythm—vv—.

Grace Darling (32)
On the coast of Northumberland, in NE England is a basaltic outcrop that
has a long avenue of history, including its being the site of the capital of
the Northern kingdom at the time of the Danish invasions.This place of
romance, chivalry and courage was the birth-place of Grace Darling
(1815-42) whose fame rests on her life-saving deed in high seas. The
rhythm of the first two verses of the poem, however stormily interpreted
should not lose the flow of ocean. With the third verse, the rhythms may
receive a more jagged, rock-like treatment, building up to an impressive
crescendo.

The lady with the lamp (33)
Florence Nightingale in the Winter of 1854/55 (34)
These two poems deal with the same theme, the first more in recitative
style, the second charged with declamation. In the latter, the second
verse—of six lines—may gain effect if spoken with a gradual
accelerando, the remaining verses resuming a firm (though not
unyielding) steady rhythm.

Striding through the land

Rosehips (36a)
Catkins (36b)
These two lyrics are for younger children. The first (36a) is predominantly —v— a rhythm that has been found to help strengthen a sense of
inner calm.

Winter in St James's Park (37a)
This park has often been experienced as a 'green' haven stretching
between Whitehall, Trafalgar Square and Buckingham Palace in the
central hub of London. Children who are studying the Industrial

Revolution may well be interested to hear of the ardent way Olivia Hill went about preserving green spaces in London for future generations and how her example was taken up in other conurbations.

Northern Lights (37b)
The choice of poetry for those who wish to find something relevant for use during an astronomy or physics main lesson is somewhat limited; this poem may serve to widen it.

Spring Showers (38)
Blackbird in Spring (39)
Sheep Bell (40)
These three poems give glimpses into different aspects of the spring season, suitable for children at various stages. The first explores the calming effect of the rhythmic transition from anapaest (vv—) to iambus (v—). The second is liberally sprinkled with the sound 'B', something that Rudolf Steiner suggested as being supportive for younger children in particular. The third moves beyond springtime. The last verse could be used, if it is felt that way, as a helpful evening verse for an individual child, but otherwise omitted in class-work.

Poised at his Eyrie (41)
Tennyson's magnificent poem, 'The Eagle' touches on a number of attributes of this almost legendary 'king of birds'. Here the intention is to culminate in the creature's intense power of sight.

In the County of Sussex (42a)
Alpine cowherd (42b)
Pine gripping granite (44)
Schaffhausen (45)
Sertsey (46a)
Teak (46b)

These five poems take us into a variety of landscapes. (42a) captures the quick-change succession that one finds in much of the English landscape. (42b) appeals to a child's love of contrast—here the craggy heights and the cultivated pastures of the mountains. (44) was inspired by seeing a solitary pine poised on the very edge of a mountain precipice. (45) personifies the Rhine as it makes its journey from Alpine heights to the North Sea. (46a) and (46b) may provide inspiring models for 12 year-olds to put some of the impressions they have gained from their geography lessons into verse form.

Discovery (47)
Sunset over the Pampas (48a)
Autumn Sunrise over the Orwell (48b)
These three poems are written in styles suitable for pupils in the Middle School, each in its own way exploring the poetic potential in the mood

of each region: the sultry equatorial rain forest (47), the invigorating plains of the South American temperate grasslands (48a), and the wide expanses of watery East Anglia just north of 'Constable country' (48b).

The flow of manhood

Flow of manhood (52a)
Saved from the storm (52b)
Salmon (53a)
Seals (53b)
Fish (54a)
The Oarsman's song (54b)
The Light-house (55a)
Fisherfolk (55b)
Anchor (56)
Viking Figure-head (57a)
A sequence of ten poems, which are all linked with the ocean in one way or another. This is a theme which the teacher often draws upon during the pupil's school career, sometimes in verse form.

Mimir's Well (57b)
Fashioning Thor's hammer (58)
The slaying of Fafnir (59a)
Sword of Sigurd (59b)
Grani (60a)
If often comes as a surprise that Norse mythology holds many treasures for 9/10 year olds, irrespective of the culture in which they have been reared. These verses are on the slender side and may be particularly suitable for classes who are learning English as a foreign language.

Breaking in (60b)
Grain Growing (61)
These two poems offer special opportunities for movement as the rhythm is regular and clear-cut: $-v-v$ alternates with $-v-$ in (60b); and $- -$ alternates with $-v-$ in (61). Even without movement such straightforward rhythms may be found supportive for the pupils at the age in which their breathing and blood circulation are becoming more established.

The Ploughman (62)
Word repetitions such as are found in this poem may be of help in establishing stability for a class of 9/10 year-olds, going through a rowdy stage.

Beowulf (63a)
For classes who need this kind of story (age 10+), but who will probably not yet be ready to recite any of the original, a few lines of this type of alliterative verse may be helpful.

Jacob's Ladder (63b)
Noah's Ark (64a)
David's Sling (64b)
As an alternative to the psalms or to the superb prose of the Old
Testament, a verse which permits the pupils to dwell in recitation with
one or other of the Old Testament stories may be a welcome feature in
the lessons.

Poems for morning and evening

Morning and Evening Verses (66-72)
It can sometimes be a great help to children in their general develop-
ment if they say a suitable verse in the family setting in the morning as
preparation for the coming day and/or in the evening as a lead into sleep.
These verses have been written with this more intimate atmosphere in
mind.

Suggested ages

The number on the left shows the page on which the poem appears. If there is more than one poem on the page the poem that appears first is listed first.

70......................................6 7 8 9 10 11
71a.....................................6 7 8
71b.....................................6 7 8 9
72......................................8 9